HOME

HOME

poems
by Jim Simmerman

Dragon Gate, Inc.

Grateful acknowledgment is made to the editors of the follow-
ing publications, in which some of these poems, often in earlier
versions, have appeared:

Antaeus: The Dead Madonnas of Santiago

Aspen Anthology: Sex

Award Highlights (Water Mark Press): Black Angel, Delusions
of Grandeur

Carolina Quarterly: The Funeral, Leaving, Places

Columbia, A Magazine of Poetry & Prose: My Parents Send a Ring
from the Bahamas

Denver Quarterly: In Her Sparse Season (The Land, section 4)

Intro 10: Something (originally titled Poem)

Iowa Journal of Literary Studies: Long Distance Bickering (Day
Rate)

The Iowa Review: A Brief Introduction, Digger, On an Uncon-
ceived Painting by Lautrec, Ricky Ricardo Drinks Alone, Soon

Midlands: My Brother's Hands

The Missouri Review: If, Spinner, What Is Wrong with This
Picture?

North American Review: Hagiography

Open Places: Winter, Your Father's House

Other Voices in American Poetry—1980: On a Black and White
Photograph of a House

Pavement: My Old Man

Quarterly West: Black Angel

Published by Dragon Gate, Inc., 508 Lincoln St.,
Port Townsend, Washington 98368

CONTENTS

A Brief Introduction, 6

I   *The Land*

On a Black and White Photograph of a House, 11
My Brother's Hands, 12
My Old Man, 13
Places, 16
My Parents Send a Ring from the Bahamas, 19
Jane, 20
The Land, 22

II   *What Is Wrong with This Picture?*

Delusions of Grandeur, 29
Epithalamion: the Ducks at Lake Lotawana, 30
Sex, 32
In the Language of Flowers, 33
Roses, 34
Leaving, 36
The Double Cherry, 37
Long Distance Bickering (Day Rate), 38
Wedding Photograph with Clock, 39
What Is Wrong with This Picture?, 41

III   *Spinner*

On an Unconceived Painting by Lautrec, 45
The Housewife Laments Her Purchase of Floating Eggs, 46
Spinner, 47
Ricky Ricardo Drinks Alone, 49

Henry, 51
Elegy in Fifths, 55
The Dead Madonnas of Santiago, 58
Digger, 60

IV   *Winter, Your Father's House*, 65

V   *Postposterous*

Something, 79
If, 81
Black Angel, 82
The Funeral, 84
Hagiography, 85
Soon, 88
To You in Particular, 90
Postposterous, 92
A Blessing, 94

for my family

A BRIEF INTRODUCTION

Oops!
Well, as long as you've caught me at it,
you may as well come in.
You are, of course, in a poem
by the talented and acclaimed poet, Simmerman.
Now, now. No need for all that.
This way, please.

Here is the poet's collection
of Jimi Hendrix and Todd Rundgren albums.
Here are his guitars, his congas, his buffoon.
Listen, you can hear the poet now,
whacking out a few "hot licks."
Not bad, eh? I mean, he doesn't spend
all his time writing, you know.

And here is where the poet keeps his narcotics:
his Ripple, his croquet mallet, his M & M's.
Please! No samples. This way.

Here we have one of the poet's
forthcoming works. Please read with me:

> A robin pecks
> at the ice
> in my rain gutter.
>
> I make a big
> deal of it.

And in this stanza, an assortment
of knockout images:
the stalled Studebaker of circumstance;
abstinence, that flaccid halo;
the rotisserie of despair.
Now really! Put that back.
What if every line-starved rhymester
pilfered a trope here, an image there?
Before long, everyone would be writing this well.

And now, what you've been waiting for,
the poet himself during a routine day.
Here he is nibbling a candy wrapper,
gulping his morning cup of smoke.
And here, lobbing turtles onto the freeway.
Here he is bicycling
through a Spanish concerto.
Here, performing *kata* on a wave.
Here we find him conducting his own funeral.
Here, carrying his head on a silver tray.
And here, if you'll join him, stepping
out of an elevator onto the Milky Way. . . .

I

The Land

ON A BLACK AND WHITE
PHOTOGRAPH OF A HOUSE

Where is the family dressed for church,
posed on the porch like manikins?
Where is the burlap welcome mat?
Where the broken wicker broom?

Where is the sober black sedan
polished to a glossy sheen,
its chrome-trimmed running boards like glass?
Where is the reflected street?

Where are the chalk scrawls on the walk—
hopscotch, two-square? Where the clouds
that drift a time as one, then break
into a harbor choked with sails?

Where are the leaves of the sycamore,
its branches bare as the wrought iron fence
that holds this house inviolate,
like memory, but holds nothing there?

MY BROTHER'S HANDS

Outside my window the branches
brush so gently I cannot hear them.
A fly rubs its legs,
scuttles the length of the sill.
Uncalled for, unexplained,
these acts so innocent
I am almost convinced. . .
But my thoughts turn
like a thief
hearing his name on unfamiliar lips.
Here, where there is no name but my own,
I think of my brother.
I see him, seven years gone.
But his eyes have grown huge
and black as a woman's.
They seem to circle me
as crows circle a wounded thing.
His mouth is drawn tight as a scar
so that I think he will never
speak with it again.
He raises his arms like a sleepwalker
and I see, for the first time,
his hands.
They are smooth and white
as the meat of an apple,
each finger a slender wand.
I imagine them poised over the keys of a piano;
rising, cupped and sure, from a stream;
leafing the pages of a Bible;
folded in sleep.
I imagine them pointing in accusation.
And I remember words, sharp as cleavers,
bearing down of their own weight.

MY OLD MAN

My old man taught me the four-beat line:
"Straighten up and fly right," he'd order,
stabbing his forefinger into my chest.
An Air Force sergeant for twenty-three years,
he never flew anything but off the handle.
I can still see his eyes bugging out
like a chow's, the veins in his neck
like a relief map of a mountain range.
Bullied his entire life by bad luck
and loss, hasty marriage, a child
he claims was three months premature,
he tried to bully respect from me.

"Pardon my French," he'd quip, farting,
his hairy belly slopping over a pair
of plaid Bermudas, the crotch ripped.
I remember him squatting in the yard
like a toad to catch the sizzling curves
I fancied I pitched. He threw them back
like a girl. And I remember the pitch
of the fast-talking carny who took
my old man, before wife and kids,
for a month's pay. He marched us home
in silence, shut himself in the bathroom.
We heard water running for hours.

"Do as I say, not as I do," he advised.
I did neither. Once, I was sentenced to
comb the yard of rocks, a hundred a day,
for a year. They got so sparse, finally,
I had to steal them from the neighbors.
I was decorated most of my childhood
with the bruises left by his "love taps."
I was double-fisted in the back of

the neck for arguing with my mother.
My old man stammered himself into rage—
that's when his hands got articulate.
He could hand-tool a belt in half
an hour flat, knock his firstborn son
unconscious, or watercolor a seascape.

At seventeen, my old man overseas, I
ran away. Shivering beneath an interstate
in Albany, afraid to sleep, I tried to
assemble the little I knew of his life
before me. The runt of a litter of six;
born in St. Louis the day his mother
died. His father never forgave him that
and palmed him off on his married sisters.
He was passed between them as casually
as a salt cellar— "A millstone and a trial."
Then, a soldier. World War II arrived
before his first whisker, and what he did,
was done to him, in the Pacific "theater"
is a bedtime story he refused to tell.

"I made a mistake," I stammered into the cold
receiver of the pay phone. "I want to come
home." In the long silence that followed,
I remembered sitting at the kitchen table
with my old man the day I demanded he
send me away to school. "Why?" he asked.
"Because," and I said it right out loud,
"I hate you." In the next five years
he didn't hit me, didn't touch me. We
coexisted like two bricks in the same wall.
When he left for Guam to load bombs, I

wouldn't even wish him luck. . . . Though now
I remember the touch of something closer.
It was my old man's voice. "Come home."

And what can I tell you, old man, turned
out on a pension of high blood pressure
and migraines, your family scattered,
the last ten years faded out like the
smoke tail from a jet? This morning,
for the umpteenth time, I listened
to your dream: to pass the last years
painting sunrises from a tramp steamer,
to watch the swells converge in distance,
to live the past as it might have been.
And so I go again among the small things—
the hackneyed words, the gestures, the brush
of a hand—which I must trust were stabs
at love. Good luck, old man. *Bonne chance.*

PLACES

For an instant
the land itself is burning
bright as an industrial park.
Then
the slow breakers of smoke.

Later
if you were there
you would have seen the aisles
of shallow graves
arranged in pairs and threes
like ebony piano keys.

When I was ten
I boiled an egg
for one whole day
then peeled away the white
and bounced the yolk
made hard as a handball.

My grandfather gave me two-dollar bills
and played the ponies
he could pick
my father claims
clean as his teeth.

In New Orleans
because of the floods
they bury the bodies above ground.
They embalm them to decay
and load them into family vaults
the size of horizontal phone booths.

Later they sweep the ashes
into a small shaft
at the foot of the vault
where there is room it seems
for three hundred years' ancestry.

My grandfather closed off
most of the three-story apartment house.
He turned the top floor into a shooting gallery.
The second he used for storage:
grandmother's furniture buried in sheets.
On the first floor he kept
one small apartment
where my Aunt Fannie lived
after each marriage failed.

My grandfather moved
his bed into the kitchen
and there he stayed
studying the racing sheets
smoking
giving tips across the phone.
He rigged the room
with strings and pulleys:
a giant web
by which to operate
the lights and appliances
without ever leaving bed.

Years after the fire
I saw a film:
an old woman climbed

into her husband's grave
and lay there refusing to move.

Where did she think she was going
calmer than an actress?
Through what door?

When I was ten
I soaked a wishbone
in a jar of vinegar.
In six days
it was resilient as rubber.

My grandfather and I
we tested it.
We saw it stretch between our hands.

MY PARENTS SEND A RING
FROM THE BAHAMAS

Because I know you know I
don't wear rings, this gift
is beyond me. I slip it

past the scarred knuckle
I put through the bedroom
window once. It looks okay

but calls to mind the tree-
climbing guitarist who lost a
finger where his ring caught.

This metal serpent further
recalls how African primitives
mold the necks of their young,

not to mention the collar
by which I found my first
dog hanging. "Just a little

remembrance," says the
note, "which you'll probably
lose like the rest." —The tie,

the watch, the hand-tooled belt.
Though this, being smaller,
should prove less difficult.

JANE

Who could recite the forty-
eight states and their capitals
in order of admission
can no longer keep straight the
names of her husband, dogs, and
children. "Jeffry," she'll yell at
the French poodle Jock who goes
on licking his haunches while
Jeffry glares at her over
his Bible, disgusted. Or
"Darry" to her husband who's
heard it too many times and
shuts himself in the bedroom.
"Darry" has left and changed his
name and never calls. Often,
in midsentence, she'll falter,
her last word a drab pigeon
falling from flight. And who can
say where her mind goes then? To
some crackerbox house in the
rubble of her girlhood? To
her dead father's hand, raised
against her in poverty
or rage? To bury her mother
one more time—or before that,
to the hospital to watch
her collapse, to read to her bleached
eyes about the many rooms
in our Father's house? Whose
father? Not mine. My father
stays in the bedroom doing
God-knows-what while Jane sets the
table for four like someone
told early on that neatness
counts, and eats alone,

while Jeffry gobbles
scriptures and teases the dogs,
while "Darry," eight hundred miles
off, scribbles and watches his
own marriage stall. And now,
I've seen it, she's falling
asleep to the drone of some
sitcom in which the simple,
good wife, through sheer gumption
and a second-rate plot, holds
her family together for
one more week, and invisible
voices laugh at the outcome.

THE LAND

James Alma Flowers, 1892-1976

1 *Alma*

A smell. A word. Whatever
takes you back there, down
the dark, broken pathway, through
the hedge, into the

yard, alone—the secret time
stolen from silence
one untranslatable night
when the shadowtag

winds came sneaking and breathing
and ruffling up
the weeds—*Alma*, your name gone
into rain, its smell

falling on freshly turned dirt.

2   Kite

I could say the rain
made me stupid
or vagrant,
the long grasses knelt
beneath the winds
of this world.

She looked so calm.

Yes, they told me
how light the jewel
box was. How they had to
practically hold it down.

I could say I'm sorry, but

that changes what?
How I dream my hands
feeding out this string?
The box open? You
soaring at the end?

Like a kite.

Your skin beginning to
stretch and shred.
Your bones folding up
like a pocketknife.

Like a pocketknife.

And the thin yellow robe
trailing from your ankles.

I could say someone's lost
his umbrella, but every
version of you
escapes me.

Dear kite, dim jewel,
I'm sorry.
I'm too far
away from you to cry,
too stupid
to keep my hands closed.

3 *Lilies*

Nothing changes here
but the stoplight at the gate,
red to green and back
every half minute, and the
flowers. The cypress
still wears its veil of Spanish
moss. The fallen leaves
still scatter like blown kisses.
This autumn I have come
with a basket of lilies
to watch the sun slip
through the arms of the elms, as
it has each evening
of the five years I've made this
call; to watch shadows
thread the disheveled yard as
if to stitch something
back together, as if to
make things whole. I tear,
one by one, the petals from
the lilies, loose them
like moths to the breeze. A few
settle on her thin
quilt of dust—she loved lilies
best, and most in fall.

4   *In her sparse season*

In her sparse season she became, like the forests,
more lovely; like the forests of her Arkansas
where she grew to believe in heaven
as that place one remembers at the last.

And she practiced at the last, beyond all things,
memory: long walks among dogwoods, hickories,
and ragged patches of light. The old herd dog with her
or gone, but not beyond calling, always coming back.

And coming back to herself, she remembered the dog
sleeping, how it would sniff the air, and stiffen,
and the faint yelp that would follow, but from a place
so gone there was no imagining it.

Nor this: she, lying before me in her yellow gown
and her blindness. So that I cannot say where it was,
that place from which she twice called out, *Who's
he going to be kin to?* —that final privacy, that home.

II

*What Is Wrong
with This Picture?*

DELUSIONS OF GRANDEUR

after Magritte

Ah, miracle beyond the snapdragon! Beyond
The plaintive timbre of seas! The body of
Woman from the body of woman grows! Blossoming
Like a fountain of candles, like a lovely face
Without ambition or shame. The season's made
Mad for it. See how the sky shocks itself
Into fissures of blue ice. How men settle back
In the gondolas of pale balloons, to drift
Beyond heat. By morning they are lost,
Filaments of thin smoke, sketching a horizon.

But if a man should touch a woman's breast,
He must dash his guitar repeatedly against
His own face. If his face bleeds, he must
Shave himself naked and walk backward into
The sea. If the sea will not keep him, he must
Drink all the hapless blood from History. He
Must memorize the shapes of clouds and learn to
Eat wind. He must fall down on his knees and beg
The earth, "Forgive me, forgive me." If the earth
Remains silent, he must touch a woman's breast.

How like the world the world is! A pure
Longing, as of a man bending to kiss
The palm of his own hand. How like
The body of woman to become water, hands
Waving from the bottoms of lakes.
This is why blood loves percussion.
Why men set loaves of bread upon
The water, and step back. This is why
We must go on and on with it,
Staring into our little bowls of hunger.

EPITHALAMION: THE DUCKS
AT LAKE LOTAWANA

for Janet

Christmas fell as scant snow
over Lake Lotawana, but we fell
harder through words. Waking to
darkness on the hide-a-bed,
I looked across the lake, to where
the lights on a dwarf juniper
blinked like fallen stars. Night
struck a less capricious sky,
but I preferred to search your face,
composed in sleep like tea leaves
in a china cup. I wanted then
to wake you with a carol, but
having lost my voice, could only
work my lips like gainless wings—
Dearly beloved, remember the ducks.

Silent night we sang all
the drunken drive from town;
headaches like tubas, knees
banging baggage like bass drums.
Then there was the story of the
pilot light that wouldn't, the man
who locked the keys inside the house.
You snapped at me. I mugged.
Christmas Eve was a coin toss
between the Mormon Tabernacle Choir
and crazy eights. I held you
stacked the deck. The hide-a-bed

was shorter than our tempers,
and cold. Though the ducks
were amused: *quack, quack.*

Ducks are regal writes a poet,
each a witness in his way. Like us,
they preen and waddle through
absurd scenes. They are suspicious.
They get too fat for their wings.
That night, I wished upon a star
and found a birthmark on your back.
You cried yourself awake. The sheet
weighed less than words. In dawn's
gray rehearsal, the juniper
gone dark, I watched two mallards
skim the lake; their bulk seemed
more than wings could bear. I
made a promise to those ducks.
They broke to thinner air.

SEX

In love, a woman will lose herself, and so
repeat the name by which she knows the man
inside her no more than a seashell knows
the irritant for which the pearl is spun.

A man repeats the alphabet or breaks
rhythm, thinking to prolong in her
the absent lap and moan from which he takes
a tinker's joy. In craft alone he's sure.

If sex *is* music, form and content slur
into the pearly script of a refrain.
Each grunt becomes a note, becomes a word
for what the body wrought but won't retain.

He blows her ear as if it were a conch.
Her fingers play his vertebrae like stops.

IN THE LANGUAGE OF FLOWERS

Like laburnum, I am forsaken.
Like fleur-de-lis, I burn.
Like the mourning bride, I have lost all.
I am a white rose, a heart ignorant of love.

Like the yew tree, you are my sorrow.
Like China rose, you are beauty's bloom.
Like wild oat, you are the witching soul of music.
You are honeysuckle, milk of the moon.

If you should ever leave me,
Alas for my poor heart!
The dandelion should be your faithful mourner.
The balm of Gilead should bloom no more.

Like black mulberry, I should not survive you.
You are crimson polyanthus, heart's mystery.
Like love-lies-bleeding, I am hopeless, not heartless.
You are a white poppy sleep, my bane, my relief.

ROSES

Asleep, you turn from me as
earlier, and awake, I turned
from you. All night I have
lain awake, searching
my heart as though it were
a book in which I hoped
to find a few pressed roses.

I found no roses. Nor would
the weary petals of sleep
enfold me. Darkness was a kind
of mirror then, circumspect
and private, returning to me
the image of a porcelain vase
broken on the carpet,
a door slamming closed.
Something within me gave,
as though from my heart,
as I have called it, a page
were being torn.

              I recited
to myself the story of
a man walking endlessly
down a narrowing street,
the houses growing sparser,
more distant, the last
lights winking out like stars.
I remembered the secret
vow of a child: one day
to leave, run far away, never
to return in this world.

In darkness, I thought
to tell you this, wide-eyed
and godless, as though the night
were a mask through which
I might speak without shame.
I thought to tell you that
the end is an autumn wind
among roses, that the lesson
of the roses is dispassion,
a final letting go. I
thought to say how words
belie roses. . . .

                    But you
were sleeping; I was talking
to myself again.

LEAVING

Today was like the sky leaving
and no one saw it but me,

how clouds cut the sun
clean of the land,

how the river kept changing
though the same reflection stayed,

how motion comes, as in a car, to
be a stillness, the still things moving.

I could have broken the river
with a stone, and all the sky

reflected there; it wouldn't have
changed the image, the instant

for which motion doesn't care,
how you turned the key and

drove away, how I watched
and stood there.

THE DOUBLE CHERRY

After you left, the sun
snapped back. That is,

a few clouds left as well.
The wind died into some

worn pocket of sky. That is,
a cherry tree stood still.

The double cherry is sweetest,
though one-per-bushel rare;

is two cherries, snared
in a lingering kiss;

is reminiscent of the heart
a child would draw. Nowhere

does one taste such sheer
amour as that of the cherry

for its twin, though each
has its own—*pit* we say

instead of *heart*, and breaks
so cleanly from its stem.

LONG DISTANCE BICKERING
(DAY RATE)

Preposterous to brood so late into love
and at such distance ("falling" thirty-two
feet per second per sec—). A few uncalled-
for words scurrying across the continent

via Schenectadys of circumlocution, already
outraced by a punctual globe (a handspin
shy of darkness or the long face of rain,
whence breaks this rumbling, neither

disconsolate god nor arpeggio, come tardy,
of illumination). How far into notion
the words spill, tailing the lightning

stab of innuendo across a protracting
gape: infinite bones to pick, infinite
points of departure riddling the heart.

WEDDING PHOTOGRAPH
WITH CLOCK

Once the figures in this photograph
    touched just so in earnest, and
      said certain words as

though they believed them, believed that the
    saying could make them so.
      The new snow that fell

that night, while they were sleeping, was a
    witness. Some clouds outside,
      where no one could see them,

reshaped themselves, and passed on.
    Once there was a woman in a
      black dress, who could walk

out of any scene written, knew it,
    and kept it to herself like
      a private account.

Once, a man in a pink oxford shirt,
    who mistook luck for a fat
      harvest moon, an

exchange of lines on a bridge one night,
    a commitment, against odds,
      to love. But you can't

say *love* in a poem and expect
    anyone to believe it,
      the way you can't kiss

a photograph each night, and ache, and
dream it all again. And the
    clock that looms behind

the young couple as they embrace—in
the snapshot, in the perfect
    past tense—the clock with

its separate hands coming together
like scissors, as if to clip
    the very lines by

which a future hung, a future yet
to be pictured or faced, an
    echo severed of

source—you can't say the clock was
then, is now, an accurate
    image of final

loss, ticking away in memory,
    where it can neither be changed
    nor made to leave off.

WHAT IS WRONG
WITH THIS PICTURE?

Halloween, 1980

It is five a.m. and the stars
are still out. Like me now,
they have nowhere to go—
no home, that door
slammed finally shut,
because the backwash of choice
is consequence
and living
with oneself. Earlier
there was a party in a room
like the world, too large
and empty for dancing. The late
hour drove a few to
touch—drove a man with a face
like the aftermath of drought,
a woman disguised as a woman
who could make it by herself.
There was a Polaroid camera
to witness it all,
and over a hundred photographs
spread across the floor—
each an attempt, for once,
to get it right,
to see the self
as *other*
in a stunned instant
of fluent light.

*

What is wrong with this
picture is always me.
Always the half-smile

made sadder by lamplight,
the mapwork of muscles
that muster a face
so tentative it would shatter
were someone to touch it,
however gently
or well-wishing.
In triple exposure, I am
they: the disparate masks
of a prior self,
equivocal
and unconvincing—
finally assembled,
finally held—
to whom I might say,
I was you once,
but am not you now
if possibility
is what the past won't admit.
So that to go home now
is to go home alone,
into the starless dawn
of my new life.

III

Spinner

ON AN UNCONCEIVED
PAINTING BY LAUTREC

Think of an apache dancer bent on
the indifferent arm of her partner
in a painting by Lautrec. Think of red
as the scarf knotted at her throat,
and of the faint impression it
will leave on her flesh. Think of
the brilliant blade of the knife
her partner used to slice the soft
clay from his boots not a half
hour before. And of the clouds
of cigarette smoke swirling
in the spotlight's beam. And
of the shadows carved into the
hardwood floor.

            In a dark corner
of the canvas, the ill-formed
artist arranges his legs and
coughs. He imagines he knows
the woman across the room, sipping
rosé through a straw. He dabs
at his mouth with the tip of his
tie and studies the line of
her neck. He imagines cutting it
with a clean red stroke, stepping
back to appreciate the slow violence
of paint drying hard.

                  Think of
night, Lautrec alone in his studio
with a box of paints and an empty
canvas. Think of the spot of red
on his tie. And of the cathedral
bells coughing out the hour.

THE HOUSEWIFE LAMENTS
HER PURCHASE OF FLOATING EGGS

after Agostini's "Open Box"

A bank of thunderclouds is gathering overhead.
If I open the box, the eggs will all float away.
Perhaps they will become trapped in the power lines,
Resembling a musical measure composed entirely of
Whole notes.
Perhaps they will be struck by lightning, exploding
Into a thick yellow rain.
Perhaps my husband,
Returning from the Motorola plant,
Will see them littering the sky above our subdivision.
A fat, golden yolk may plop against his windshield,
Sliding down the glass like a plump snail.

But what if the eggs should catch in a skydiver's parachute,
Thwarting his descent, spiriting him away?
What if a goldfinch mistakes one of the eggs for her own,
Perching atop it as it pops into the clouds?
And if she mistakes the skydiver's parachute
For a nest?
The skydiver, looking down, will see the earth
Receding like a brass doorknob.
My husband, looking up, will see a single goldfinch
Gliding beneath a skydiver's parachute,
Or the soles of a pair of boots
Disappearing into rain.

SPINNER

for Michael Pfeifer

Consider the eyes
gone deeper than holes.
They contain the black
heat of matches,
extinguished,
just before they smoulder.
The hair pulled back
in awkward knots
and bound with a rag,
as though excess
were somehow contemptible,
and beauty itself
an affront.
And yet there is beauty
in the pinched lips
which refuse speech
the way certain rocks
refuse color.
There is beauty
in the cheap buttons
missing from her blouse,
perhaps stitched
to a worn stocking
stuffed with rags—
a crude doll
discarded with childhood
in a clapboard shed
above the river.

Now she is like the river,
a raw testament
closing itself

in the icy lap of winter.
She is like the gray light
reflected there,
which is the aftermath
of beauty,
which redeems nothing.
Not even the solemn
face of a girl
who stood there once,
touching the patches
of blood on her skirt
and praying for night
to swallow its billion stars.
Stars so animate,
so futile—
like spools
played out of thread.
Like the empty wheel
spinning furiously now
through her hands,
glistening
with a dark oil,
that would be hard
and warm
if you could touch them.

RICKY RICARDO
DRINKS ALONE

I-yi-yi-yi! look at that moon
floating up there like a teaspoon
of sweet cane sugar or the head
of a conga drum. Someone said
the man in the moon is an old
Cuban fisherman who sold
his boat for enough bay rum
to sail out of his body one
soft Havana night, and half
the time I think it's true. Laugh
if you like, but I have watched
his eyes fix upon the thatched
hat of a woman who waits
each night by the dock for her late
sailor to return, only to
see the morning paint a blue
and emptier harbor, only to turn
once more from the sea and yearn
slowly home, across fallow
tideland. Her long yellow
dress made her look, from
a distance, like a canary, come
to sing the forests back.

              What
has become of the rain that cut
through the night like maracas? And
of the flower monger whose hand
was a warm garden on my neck? And of
the sails that hovered like doves
on the horizon? And of the clop-
clop-clop of Lucinda? I want to stop
the moon with a bray sometimes. I
want to bray so sweetly it will fly

backward, like an empty bottle
over my shoulder. Bray until
I am back on the beach with my
father, learning to tie
a bowline, mend a net. There
was a song he sang—I remember
how the surf beat out time, though
the words, the words. . . Low
tide left me shells shaped like
pink fans. Luck was the bright
bit of glass I found one day. Keep it
close, he told me. Memory is a ship
in a bottle. The bottle breaks.

HENRY

I worked the kitchens
of all the good restaurants:
the Steak House, the Gables,
the—what you call it?
Granny's now;
used to be the Lumberjack.
And clean.
I would wear my whites,
pull a seven, eight hour shift—
not a spot. Nothing.
Never smoked in the kitchen.
Never let anyone else.
"There is a station," I would say,
"go smoke over there."
I stood side by side
with the best ones: Angel,
he is in Gallup now;
Alonzo, out at the country club.
I was born here,
spent most of my life here.
How old you think I am?
Fifty next month.
I am—how you say it?
Pescado, the fish.
I am always swimming
and breathing the water.
Place next door
used to be a bakery.
Real bread, real tortillas.
That was when Joe,
the first Joe,
opened this bar.
A real man, that Joe.
Times no one had any money

we all drank free here.
He gave us elk meat and cigarettes.
Everyone sang.
Things were different then.
Trains used to run more often.
You could go anywhere
for fifty dollars.
I quit school in eleventh grade,
followed a girl to California.
She was beautiful. Chicana,
you know, but like you:
light skin, curly hair.
I loved that girl.
But she died on me.
Car wreck.
Maybe I am stupid,
but sometimes I cry.
Because I see her
like she was,
and I reach out
to hold her,
and she is not there.
Some people say it is alright;
she is with the big guy,
the Lord, up above.
But how can she be there
when she is still in here?
And if she is in here,
nothing can replace her.
It is like you die too,
in a way.
You go on talking,
and smoking, and drinking all night,
but it is not you really;

just a body you live in
like a rented room.
That is when I left
for the army.
Didn't come back
for four years.
Then I had money—
five thousand dollars.
You should have seen me:
three hundred dollar suits,
forty dollar shoes.
And still I got in fights.
The cowboys.
They would be working for the Babbitts;
forty dollars a week.
I would steal their girls.
I was something really.
Jojo had bought the bar by then.
He let me stay in the basement.
All the time—card games, dice.
Some of us are born lucky,
you know, swimming.
I worked the best restaurants.
And every night—the smoking,
the drinking, the women,
the fights.
There are no good restaurants now.
They freeze the fish.
They burn the meat.
And so I am not working.
Now I only smoke
when I drink.
Sometimes I go five,
six weeks without a cigarette.

But the only way to quit
is to do it.
Stop. Pfft, like that.
And still, I remember the girl,
and I cry.
I am not much of a man.
It is stupid, you know,
the way things change
and do not change
all at the same time.
Like some of us are little fishes
swimming around and around
in a glass bowl.
And we do not know
it is not the ocean.
And we do not want to stop.
And so I am Henry,
the little fish,
stupid, but lucky
to be talking to you
on the other side of the glass.
Let me buy you a drink
out there, where the air is good,
and free, and invisible.
Let me borrow a match.

ELEGY IN FIFTHS

for J.L.T.

Now she's dead.
Now she's important.
I have to get off the couch
to answer the phone
to listen to this.
I have to be surprised
at the voice of an old heartthrob
and give a damn
about her paper-making and marriage.
Outside, the pines I cut yesterday
clutter the yard and need splitting.
On television, twenty-two men
bash each other's skulls in for money.
It's Sunday.
My neighbor knots up for church.
My dog rolls over and plays dead,
and I have to scratch her belly.

★

I don't want to hear how the car
veered slowly to the right,
implying booze
or calculation.
I don't want to hear
how the pole went down,
disrupting calls for a square mile,
or how she was putting
her life in order.
I don't want to hear some bird
whistling for the hell of it.
Or the kids next door

fighting for window seats.
I don't want to hear myself
being sad and sincere
to a piece of black plastic.
I don't want to hear it.

★

Naturally life, as we call it,
goes on,
but we don't say how
or to what end.
Naturally, the mind
slips into reverse,
and I'm back there
changing her tire again.
What would I give
to have been in the car
beside her, as I was that night
the tread blew,
and I grabbed the wheel
and we lived?
What would I give
for the world's spent light?
And to whom, and what with?

★

That was St. Louis,
where anything can happen.
That was the past,
which is spilt milk,
which is a monstrous thing to say.
Still, I fumble for words

like keys
to doors that never open.
Still, recall the locks
of golden hair,
that were only dead cells,
that were lovely anyway.
Now, she moves in memory,
a garden of glass roses,
and a glass sun lights her way,
and time blows past like a tuneless hymn. . . .

I know I'm only talking.

                    ★

But once, we got so drunk
we broke
into a hotshot architect's home
and stole a bottle
of his rarest champagne,
and drank to the world
we'd outwitted,
and christened the empty road.
Now, I drink the sober facts
alone, and pray
to a god I won't believe in—
until the earth gives up
its giddy laugh,
until the broken things
reassemble themselves,
until the words disappear
in the order they were written.

THE DEAD MADONNAS
OF SANTIAGO

What words have I for the dead
madonnas of Santiago,
their eyes like smoke in rainfall?
On Palm Sunday they stir
in that half hour,
half-breath
when the moon is a chalice
of blood
tipped to the world's lip.
By torchglow
they follow narrow paths
out of the mountains,
their earrings flashing,
their full hips swaying like wheat
before a storm.
They wind into the hushed
streets of the village,
a procession
of murmurs:
Christe eleison.

Once a year they come like this,
like banished lepers,
to dip from the cool waters
of the living,
to fill the heavy stone jars
we leave by the well.
They bear them upon their heads
back into the mountains,
to their children
who wait
with the thirst of the dead.
And if, laboring

beneath the weight of her gift,
one stumbles,
soaking her long braids,
her skirt,
puddling the parched earth,
what has been lost
is nothing,
is not a drop.

DIGGER

Mainly I work at night
because there's one kind
of hole deserves all
the dark it can swill.

A person might call
the world that much lighter
for it. But I say
it's nothing so black

can't get a little blacker.
Like there was shadows
piled up behind shadows.
The first shovelful is

soft and clingy, about
the size of a baby's head.
I seen them go down too.
And the old ones,

so whittled by the time
they get here, you half
expect them to blow away,
like dried-up feathers

off the grille of a sedan.
But it's the digging
I crave—the way
the shovel takes

so natural to the land,
damp and close
as the place
between my sister's legs.

Or the times I'd make
her take me in her mouth—
it feeling how rain looks
in a fresh-dug grave.

That's her yonder,
where I put her myself.
Because that's respect.
Not only the doing

but the staring
flush at what you done.
Like looking back
over your fields

after a day's plowing
to check if your rows
are straight. Back
on the farm I'd dig

for the sweat and hell
of it. Plant a penny
to see if it would grow
into a luck tree.

I buried my sister's cat
alive. That was when
folks took care of their own.
That was family.

So that some nights,
belly-deep into
what I do best,
I can hear their voices

floating up like mist
off the marshes,
thanking me,
saying how I buried them

deep and good,
how a body couldn't want
to get buried better.
Because when the spit

and gnawing go away,
what are you
but a tatter of compost,
a name that gets mumbled

into a mouthful of dirt?
It's no stone
nor grieving
going to ask you back.

No, it's the digging
is all, standing upright
at the finish
so as to feel

the breeze skittering
through the grass
and tickling
the top of your hair.

It's the kneeling down
and setting your lips
to the ground, kissing
its cool underbelly,

whispering into it
the way night
whispers off into the trees.
Because a hole

can keep a secret,
keep whatever you give it.
It goes on down-sinking,
getting stiller and deeper,

settling in
like a grudge,
like the earth was nothing
but a worn-out brain,

and you just
helping it forget.
So that the filling-in
later is restful,

like patting a dog
or tamping down shag.
Nothing to mark
but a blister of sod,

and the shovel
sticking up out of it
like a cross
with roots instead of arms.

IV

Winter,
Your Father's House

WINTER, YOUR FATHER'S HOUSE

1   *Reasons for staying in, 12/21/75*

Drifts so high you could break your leg
on a stump if you didn't know where

you were going. Busted fence post,
buried line of barbed wire.

You could follow a set of tracks
across a creek, hit a flaw

and they wouldn't find you till March.
Or a storm could blow up suddenly

to where the horizon blurred out so
you wouldn't know sky from ground.

Another thing, going off by yourself
like that, you start remembering things

you shouldn't. Start thinking things
could be different than they are.

2 The pond, 8/64

Different how? Suppose there was a pond
where, as a kid, you used to blast

tin cans and chips of bark,
popping them clean off the water—

the pond, the day itself
set to rocking in the after-lull.

Whatever moved became target
to reflex—bird, stray dog,

any shadow, your own
reflection in the pond. Suppose

in the flat shade of evening,
you heard your father whistling

you home. Suppose you aimed
in the direction of the house.

3 *The house, 1965–3/5/72*

In the dim flurries of late-night
television, you can learn all you need to

about winter in the country—a man
lost in a blizzard shoots his dog

for food. In the same blue light
you can watch your father burrow

deeper into his nest of blankets,
deeper into his own dim conclusion.

You can watch his face turn
still and blank, like a pond

on a moonless night. Watch it
aimlessly, for years, as the wind chips

at the shingles and the house settles
into land. Watch it harden to ice.

4   *Eulogy, 3/6/72*

Because why not. Because you try
to be your father's son and hold

back the words till they choke you.
Because even a dog drags itself off

into the bushes and beats down
a place in the grass. Because

damned if you do and damned if you don't
and damned if you beg to differ.

Because dirt won't remember you.
Fire won't remember you.

Because winter is deaf
and ice is blind. Because

silent and sorry are two
cents to close your father's eyes.

5   *A story, 3/8/72*
      (recalled from 1924)

"I remember when your dad and me
was kids growing up, must have been

forty, forty-five years back. Your
dad would get up first every morning,

still dark out, and scoot
down to the barn to milk.

This one morning it got so cold
your dad's ears froze. (He never

would wear no hat.) Doctor
said you could have flicked them with

a finger and they'd have busted off.
You should have heard your dad yelling

when the feeling come back. And of course,
he never heard right after that."

6   *The dream, 1972–1975*

You shout and shout, but no one answers.
The snow is so deep, you can't

lift your legs to step. The wind
keeps blowing up, and gusts

of new snow have already buried
your tracks. You strike a match;

it sputters and dies.
You strike again. A third time.

This one flares, but you drop it—
your fingers clumsy with cold.

But this snow burns, and a small drift
ignites. The wind catches it, and drift

after drift explodes into fire. A world
of snow, burning, night after night.

7   *Legacy, 3/5/75 . . .*

Twenty-four acres of land to outlast you.
Nine hundred stumps and one bonfire

worth of fence. A gutted barn
full of shovel heads and buckets;

a horseshoe for luck. The charred
skulls of cattle. A spent match.

All the bitter cold you can weather
and the animal instinct to do

just that. Nine good fingers
on which to count blessings.

The rest of your life to forget—
your father's house,

his silence, his eyes
staring in at every window.

8   *From a letter, 12/21/75*
   (dated 1/3/70)

"It's how I am mainly, brought up
never to say you are sorry or think

maybe you were wrong. So there are
maybe things I never told you that

I should have, though not saying them
doesn't make them not so.

A man can't go on blaming himself
for what he isn't, thinking how

he might have been different,
or better, which he can't know

any more than he could go back and
change if he did. It's the blood,

and it is in you sure
as hunt is in the dog."

9   *Solstice, 12/21/75*

Fold the letter. Open the door.
Break knee-deep into new snow.

Track your shadow like something
getting away, the sun a raw eye

on your neck—don't touch it.
Trace the ridge past where the cow

misstepped and broke her leg.
Past a circle of fresh tracks.

Past the headstone in its white
collar, and the last stray cracks

of day. Step out onto the frozen
face of the pond, as if

nothing has happened.
As if nothing ever will.

V

Postposterous

SOMETHING

Between space and light
Something so like the slow snap of dusk
When a woman can walk away from you
Between two trees
And never be seen again
Something poised
In the shadows of wings
Where a name is no help
Where the pointless words die down awhile
And walls release their birds
Something like the shadow of a bird
Beating against a curtain
A log revolving slowly
On a lake
Something beyond "things"
Beyond the dazzling propellers of light
Spinning suddenly out of darkness and
Gone
Beyond the spasm of an eye
In its final eclipse
Something that persists
A foolish twig
Caught in a woman's hair
The long corridors down which a man
Still wanders
The muffled sobs
Filtering through each closed door
The silhouette of a woman
Combing out her long wet hair
Something moving through the high reeds
Circling   closing
The incessant chant of rain
That enters a room

Before a man can
Close the door behind him
This chain of paper lanterns
And the wind picking up
Blowing them free and over the lake
Searchlights on the water
Baubles for the drowned

IF

on learning of a friend's miscarriage

I'm sorry. I'm not sorry. I'm not thinking
how swells blossom and break beyond
the horizon of this letter I'm not rereading
again. Or how the sun burns through the morning
haze. Or how the heart, weighed against
a feather, floats like a bubble of air.

Sometimes, when the sky is like this, like
ghost-water, I think we have already drowned
in private oceans. And I want one
white feather to stand upright on the neck of
that wave, breaking off that pier, where
a woman is waiting beneath a blue umbrella,
her ankles touching like paper orchids.

If is the emptiest cradle I know, but
I stand it, rocking here like a moored boat,
humming a scrap of lullaby: *When the*
wind blows and sailboats sheer to open
sea, their sails swollen with wind, with
light, I feel a needle work toward heart's
north, but no home to get back to.

BLACK ANGEL

There is a cemetery I walk to
in the stiff breath of autumn,
in the lengthening sequence
of dwindling days, where
the bald knolls and hollows
fold in on one another, hide
one thing from the next:
the yew tree from the crepe myrtle,
the garland from the path,
the hole in the land from
the hole in the heart—
I walk there to hide myself
from myself.

       And still
I come stark halt upon
the monument people call
Black Angel—black as a shadow
in deep water, big as a man;
and I wonder, as some must,
drawn again
into its sunken glare,
who would raise such a memory
to himself, to another,
to break from the grave's
belly of snow and stare
the living down, to say
the dead are dead
and don't come back.

       Each
night I wrestle my own
black angel, who comes upon me
like a sudden mirror,

so that I can feel the black
wings wrenching my shoulders,
see the black lips broken
by desire, by grief—
neither worse, nor less
than my own—so that
I must wrestle each night
until I am exhausted enough
to wake, to walk back
into the world of things
as they are, one step
and its consequence
after the next.

THE FUNERAL

Four minstrels in blackface
carry me in.

I seem to be wearing a red *gi*.
I seem to be hugging a small silk pillow
on which someone has embroidered
Poor Jim's a-cold.

I feel pretty natural.

My barber is there.
And some others I don't recognize.
They've all brought animals instead of flowers,
animals with bright glass eyes.

The service is conducted by a ventriloquist.
A few words muttered in French:
On n'a jamais assez . . . assez . . .
Malheureusement.

A sad little tune drifts up from the street.
Everybody hums along.
I want to thank them all for coming.
Especially the girl
in the China blue dress
who asks for an encore.

I am wrapped in a quilt.
A bowl of milk is placed at my feet,
a few rose petals floating there.

Everyone leaves through different doors.

HAGIOGRAPHY

". . . you have the feeling of sorrow, but not sorrow itself."
Ira Sadoff, "The Revolution of 1905"

ten feet closer to nothing
the bibles are still zipped tight
the faucet spits prolifically
ice cubes melt in shawls of muck
similarly you occur
you sit in your body
astounded by teeth
by fingertips
by the shadow cowering at your feet
for years it has been like this
you and your body
two survivors
adrift with provisions for one
you tried talking things out
between yourself
making offhand remarks
in the second person
you tried to throttle a wink
when everything failed
you stayed up late
picking splinters from your heart
as one by one
your ribs disappeared
when the door finally opens
like the lungs of a drowning man
you walk out on yourself
you stumble past the footprints
scrawling from your porch
past the files of bolted homes
and the river abducting itself
for three days you lie
in an open grave

watching clouds blister and peel
until your hands are clean
as unwritten scrolls
and the rains flush you up
you indulge in contortions of guilt
confess to a ruthless dependence
on water and arson
to the recurring suspicion that yes
you are a holy man
when a chorus of lights does not ensue
you feel betrayed
you feel like the last tool
of an extinct race
until it occurs to you that this
is another way of placing yourself
at the spine of things
that you are arbitrary as any fact
that salvation is a tuft of feathers
fluttering from a barbed wire fence
you remove the feathers
fold them in a silk scarf
press them to your chest
you bear yourself home
only to find the door open
the lock unchanged
beneath the porch
you discover a cache of bones
you spend the day
whittling them into straws
and when the sun is tucked away
like a bright scarf
you dream of yourself as a statue
skating the rim of a whirlpool

waking
you weave the straws into a nest
in which you lay the parcel of feathers
you bury it in your yard
sleep over it
now you dream you are an eskimo
your family thinks you dead
they bury you in a block of ice
and push you out to sea
you watch the backs of their hoods
recede like small suns
but waking
things are still the same
the malleable ears
the snake coiled inside your throat
looking back
you barely notice
the smell of burning feathers
the ashes on your tongue
your life begins to crystallize
like the first grain of salt
in the eye of Lot's wife

SOON

I will take an orange and move
into the closet. I will deposit
a small jar of water outside
the door. I will stroll the floor

of my closet like a sundial
on a cloudy day. And I will say
to myself, "Poor Mutton, now you
not hurt no one no more. Poor

wind whipping through the hair
of a corpse." As if remorse
were a fop in a
Restoration play. I

could live inside a closet if
I wanted to, even one haunted
by the remnants of no person
I had been. I could scream

like the darkness on both sides
of my skin; I could grin
like water, and no one would
check the door. I could store

a year's worth of sleep among
the teeth of a comb, or hone
it to a fine point of abstraction
and stab myself awake. Take,

for example, the water in the
jar, how it drinks itself more
out of habit than thirst. Take
the one thing a man has done

alone his entire life and
shake it like a rug; shake it
until the air begins to clot
with dust, until it becomes just

one more reverie in form,
a closet full of soot, a lull
in the lull of waiting. I will
peel my orange as the door hinge

locks with rust. I will hold my
head and sing myself a lullaby. I
will think of heaven, an empty
shelf. I will forgive myself.

TO YOU
IN PARTICULAR

No, this is no voice
from a fiery bush.
But it's something.
It is the paper boat
an orphan makes
and buries
in someone's yard.
It is the promise
made by starlight
in a story
so old
the words have worn
to a threadbare music
that is faith,
though the promise
is forgotten.
No one wants to talk
about miracles anymore.
No one wants to walk,
alone, through the dark
part of town
and kiss the withered hand
of a drunk who might be
anybody's child,
who might be most
of what is given us
to know of love
and the anguish
of Abraham.
As far as I know
the heart
is a paper boat
burning underground.
As far as I know

the world
is a broken promise,
a story
that doesn't know
how to end itself.
But who can say, really—
if the telling is good,
if the words are clear
and strong—
that it is not the voice
of God
speaking, this once,
like a very lonely man
to you in particular?
The knife is in your hand.

POSTPOSTEROUS

Alright.
I'll change my life.
Or the world at least.
I'll go back to where the plot
line snarled,
or farther maybe,
to where the first face
in the first mirror
I ever looked away from
betrayed me,
and take a half step to the left.

I was walking in the cemetery the other day
with my friend Peter,
and even that
egregious metaphor
couldn't snuff the wisecracking entirely.
Even the smallest
poem I ever read, which was a hangnail
of a headstone, which was
BABY,
couldn't make me wish
the sky smaller or darker,
the conversation less frivolous,
the big words—
I mean the really big ones:
despair and his whole squad of goons—
more singular and monolithic.

Henceforth,
I'm going to treat everyone—
and I'm including the bum
in pantyhose,
passed out and pissing on himself

in a ritzy suburb of D.C.—
as if he were the very live and very short
and mortal John Keats.

That's right. John Keats,
punching in at the foundry
and hacking into his sleeve.
Keats ahead of me in the check-out line
swapping food stamps for powdered milk
and a half-dozen pens. . . .

Because the world
is a vale of soul-making
if you think about it, and gravity
a lame excuse
for not sprouting wings on a given day.
Because woe's a lousy
mnemonic device,
as any dope could figure out
given two mirrors
and time its way.

This morning I turned Monet's "Poplars"
upside down. I mean,
life's a medley
isn't it?

You also may be amusing to know.
I'm dusting the urn as I say this.

A BLESSING

As I understand it
Dowdall drove the car

and swapped a pint
of cheap hooch

for a bird
the size of a Hoover.

L.T. held it
in the back seat

and was shat upon
for his trouble.

Fisher got a haircut
and rode shotgun.

Crowley and I
were at the Branding Iron

scarfing omelets
and chicken-fried steak.

Reser was in Missouri
and the train

that hied him off
was already grinding

through cold New England,
sailing a smoky question mark

over maimed fields
of glittering frost.

★

As I understand it
the neck was snapped

and pulled apart
as simply as a party favor.

The body hung
upside down for a day

to bleed, as far
above the snapping jaws of dogs

as a star, if you believe
that sort of thing,

above a manger.
In the interim,

Fisher was Oregon-bound,
his first family Christmas

in umpteen years.
Crowley caught cold.

The rest of us
huddled in Joe's Place

buying each other time
and beer.

It was the night before Christmas,
as far as it goes;

where we were going
was nowhere quick.

★

As I understand it
the goose was named Death,

and this is its carcass
slaughtered for meat.

Death, our collective goose, cooked
and carved

and the smell is sweet.
If we bow our heads now

it is not out of shame
nor hunger

for those we miss.
It is not out of some

predilection for rite—
the tinsel of commerce,

the claptrap of church.
If we bow our heads now

it is only to draw
more closely together,

each unto each,
the family

we've made of ourselves
and are,

gathered for now
and what it's worth.

The son of a career Air Force sergeant, Jim Simmerman grew up in Colorado, Arkansas, Alabama, Missouri, Massachusetts and England.

He attended the University of Missouri, where he received a B.S. in Education and an M.A. in English, and the University of Iowa, where he received an M.F.A. through the Writers' Workshop and a black belt in Shorinryu karate.

Currently, he resides in Flagstaff, Arizona, and teaches in the writing program at Northern Arizona University.